NOTES

ON LOVE

AND COURAGE

Hugh Prather

Notes
on Love
and Courage

Illustrations by Eugene A. Smith

Doubleday & Company, Inc.
Garden City, New York

OTHER BOOKS BY HUGH PRATHER:

Notes to Myself (diary)

I Touch the Earth, the Earth Touches Me (diary)

Wipe Your Face, You Just Swallowed My Soul (allegory)

(The novel referred to in this book is entitled *Dreams Left Burning*.
It will not be published before 1978.)

Library of Congress Cataloging in Publication Data

Prather, Hugh.
    Notes on love and courage.

    I. Title.
PS3566.R27N6   818'.5'407
ISBN 0-385-12772-3
Library of Congress Catalog Card Number 77—75873

20   19   18

*To my father
and to my mother*

To the reader:

In one sense this book is about the old values: unselfishness, loyalty, honesty, forgiveness, courage—those qualities that traditionally have been thought to be the elements of character in a good person. I didn't know this would be one of its themes. When I went back to see what I had been putting in my diary during the time I had been writing my first novel, I found I had been in a process of reclaiming much of what I had discarded when I was younger. This was surprising because the novel was, among other things, an expression of a deeply felt cynicism. At the same time as I had, with great pleasure, been turning things upside down, another part of my mind had been putting them right side up.

When I was growing up I was taught that to do good was not enough; one had to be good, and I was told that if a person was good, that is, if to the best of his ability he was gentle, honest, patient, forgiving, he would have reached the highest state possible for him to reach on this earth. The assumption—that goodness could be sought—was not questioned. If one wanted to be more loving, and if he practiced, if he labored, if he made love the focus of his life, he would, with certainty, become more loving. In so far as I am able to judge my inner state at that time, I did become a better person. I was more solicitous of other people's happiness, more generous, more willing to give up time. I saw more of the beauty in other people and in the world. And I believe this happened largely because I worked at it.

When I entered business, I saw my boyhood ideals being put to use. I was told they were practical. Sincerity was convincing, a pleasant disposition was good public relations, to be nonjudgmental (to think positively) was a powerful tool that could transform one's salesmanship from impotence to dynamism. So that the time came when even the mention of words such as cheerfulness, unselfishness, humility, courtesy, good, evil became sickening to me. I not only stopped believing in their value, I stopped believing in their possibility. Cheerfulness was phony, unselfishness was self-deceptive, humility was a weakness, courtesy was a form, and there was no such thing as good or evil.

Prejudice is blind even when it is prejudice against words. It is to me significant that so many religious teachers and prophets spent so much of their time simply urging people to be good, urging them to turn from that which destroys to that which heals. Were they wasting their time? If it's true that a human cannot improve through his own efforts, then they were wasting their time; for what is gained by firing a man's will if some predetermining principle ordains his progress? Or if mankind's deepest urges are not positive, they were wasting their time. Any influence they had would eventually be undone. Or if there is no goodness, if it doesn't exist even as a potential, they were wasting their time. They were merely pointing in all directions at once.

Goodness as form—as a hypocritical, unfelt duty—is not goodness. Goodness as a sentence, or as words spoken from a dais, or essays in an embossed volume, or as rules that can be taught, or as the unstated sanctions of a group, is not goodness. But there is goodness. Every fiber in us knows the worth of our lives. Not that we can't be bullied or deceived, not that we don't have complexes and unreasonable doubts, not that we haven't been ill-treated—we have in fact been damaged. But still we know the worth of our actions. We know what we strive for.

Hugh Prather

March 30, 1977
Santa Fe, New Mexico

NOTES

ON LOVE

AND COURAGE

Are there any wholly useless encounters? I know this: there are no insignificant people. There is no one who isn't supposed to be there.

We need other people, not in order to stay alive, but to be fully human: to be affectionate, funny, playful, to be generous. How genuine is my capacity for love if there is no one for me to love, to laugh with, to treat tenderly, to be trusted by? I can love an idea or a vision, but I can't throw my arms around it. Unless there is someone to whom I can give my gifts, in whose hands I can entrust my dreams, who will forgive me my deformities, my aberrations, to whom I can speak the unspeakable, then I am not human, I am a thing, a gadget that works but has no ashes.

We talked again last night. What he doesn't seem to realize
is that if he isn't loyal to someone, if there isn't someone
his guts will simply not allow him to manipulate, then his
life is going to be a succession of discovered deceits. His
treacheries are so reasonable that he thinks any understanding
friend would forgive him. But he will not be forgiven. Time
and again he will be abandoned. Loyalty is not reasonable.
It is the easiest sentiment of all to argue against. If we
have a friend we sometimes act against our own best interests.
A time may come when we appear quite self-destructive because
we have this friend and there is something we must do for him.
There are worse things than losing money, losing position,
even than losing life; and if we have a friend we can sense
that. But what words could I use that would reach inside him
and trigger such a feeling? I couldn't explain why anyone
would want to be that way, when he knows that he has the
alternative of acting rationally and living an orderly life.

Is your first responsibility to yourself? The question is misleading; that is, it misleads the person who takes it to heart. It's like asking, must you shift your weight in order to walk. Of course you must, but anyone who concentrates first on shifting his weight will not walk well.

There are people whose feelings and well-being are within my influence. I will never escape that fact.

Individual growth can't take precedence over relationships; it can't because it ceases to be growth in the attempt.

"Love thy neighbor as thyself" does not imply, as I have heard stated so often, that one must first love himself. It implies nothing more complicated than the fact that anything less than love is not love. Love does not exclude, it embraces. If a person doesn't love something outside himself, then very simply he does not love himself.

Is love in me, or is it something apart from me that works through me? I can reason either way, but I can't deny how it feels: it feels as if there are times when I am more myself than at others. When I love spontaneously, when it simply comes out and there is no pretext or calculation, I don't feel like either a container of some precious but foreign spirit, or like a vehicle for a thing outside of me. I feel: that which loves is me. And when the impulse is to hurt and I follow that, I feel like a betrayer, and the I has gone out of me.

To separate out my relationship to myself and set it aside for more luxuriant attention may be pleasurable, it may even be useful, but like any surgery it becomes more dangerous the longer it lasts. I am immobilized and temporarily severed from the other half of life. Ultimately my character is defined by the quality of my sensitivity to other people. I exist in equilibrium. I am here to the degree I am there.

I had not known what if feels like to be lonely until about
two years after my divorce. I was back in college then and
there was a woman in one of my classes who was very bright
and considerably overweight. We became friends. She would
throw open her vast shimmering mind and I would wade in,
totally awed. One day we were standing in the psychology
building, talking, and she reached up and very gently took
a twig or something out of my hair. It was the way she did
it. "You like me don't you, as a friend?" she said. I
said yes. "And you're divorced and unhappy and you wish
you had someone to sleep with." I said that was true.
"But you don't want to sleep with me because I'm too heavy."
"Well," I said, "I suppose that's right." "Don't you see
what you're keeping yourself from?" she said. "Tell me,
how much better are you willing to let your life become?"
But I didn't answer, because I was very young and had not
yet learned just how much someone who loves you can offer.

I can't be found in myself; I discover myself in others. That much is clear. And I suspect that I also love and care for myself in others.

This simple pattern keeps recurring: A friend tells me of a problem he has or of some misery in his life. I listen, or together we talk it out. Later I remember that I had been depressed, or not feeling well, before we met. The ailment is not only forgotten but discarded.

I spent the day being an heir. I had decided that no matter what else I did I would try to stay conscious of everything agreeable sent my way. Much has been written on the benefits of giving; I wanted to see what it would feel like to be a devoted receiver. It was pleasant. At times I felt like a person of great beauty. There was a flood of gifts from the New Mexico desert: storm clouds, birds, light on the mountains, and one rather gaily colored, though unassertive, winged something that walked in front of my cereal bowl. I wasn't surprised by most of that. What I hadn't expected was how much people in general appeared to be offering, especially people I didn't know. There is a natural outpouring from the human nature, more deliberate and sustained than I had noticed before. It comes in the form of gestures and looks and a certain endeavor in the voice, as well as outright good humor and helpfulness. It's an attitude that is often instinctive when one person is in the presence of another, and it is recognizably apart from the usual posturing. I am reminded of how some animals always stay close enough that at any time they can brush against each other.

I have a friend who is a good listener. If I tell her about some difficulty I'm having, I never get the feeling she is doing little more than waiting to say something supportive. Her primary concern is not to put on a show of being a good listener, but rather it is as though my problem has become her problem in all respects. She is intensely loyal and yet she doesn't automatically criticize the one I may be blaming. She has an instinct for knowing how much I love that person, and if I do she speaks gently because she is for me; by that I mean she wants for me what I want at the deepest level, and she knows when my anger is superficial. However, if the person is not significant to my life, her criticism so devours him that by the time she is through I can laugh at my foolishness for having exaggerated his importance.

After he told me that his younger brother had been knifed
and his eyes seemed to be pleading with me to do something
to comfort him, I spent fifteen or twenty minutes giving
him the thoughts that had helped me at times when I had
suffered. Then he said, "If my brother dies I will die at
the same moment. That's how close we are." I felt foolish
for having tried to solve things. There is a kind of pain
that is very far beyond words, and I was too busy being
conscientious to notice it. He simply wanted someone to
be with.

This day has been magical. I have been with three friends, one at a time, and I have learned that friends can transform you. The first held me up so I could see. I was able to distinguish the points where things touch, and where they divide, the essential forms coming at me from the future, new elements and consummations, and the old principles that must not be neglected. I could name them all. They spilled from my mouth. He was delighted with my concepts. He didn't seem to realize that he was the one who had given me the vision. My second friend made me gentle and earnest. She needed to talk, and so we talked for a long time. She thanked me for my concern as I was leaving, but she wouldn't have recognized me if I had been any other way. The third friend turned me into a clown, a gesturer, a creator of quips. I hadn't known my life was filled with so much absurdity. He laughed and laughed because he had made me so funny. My friends don't know what they have done today. It's nothing to them: they do it so often. I expect I must also cause a change in them. And so we—each a separate we—exist only in each other's presence. That is something precious, enough so not to walk away from easily, and something that has to be included in any definition of self-sufficiency.

Today at lunch Joe told me that he and Ann had decided to get married in three weeks. "That makes the engagement as long as the courtship." I found myself liking the absurd symmetry of that as much as Joe did. What I didn't like was what he said next: "I've never met anyone quite like her; she has everything I could possibly want." He was filling in all the blanks. I have seen so many marriages and even friendships end when the inevitable realization comes that something was left out of the other person. Sometimes nothing more tangible can be cited than the vague feeling that "something was missing." Usually it can be pinpointed: "She thought sex was a bore" or "He was humorless, totally humorless." Darleen once said to me, "Jim and I never talk books. If I want to talk books I visit Aunt May. Aunt May reads." So simple. It takes five to ten people to make up the one got-it-all friend we are all looking for.

Something within me knows that most of what I am will die without people, and it doesn't behave itself quietly. So I eventually surrender my seclusion and walk out the door. However, when the mind is given a problem to solve, its tendency is to select and fixate. That works well in a shoe store. But if I allow myself to become convinced that simply because a person is there, obvious and convenient, I am therefore in need of him, that if I don't make it with this individual I will be friendless, I not only create the likelihood that I will be disappointed, but I also scare off the very person whose companionship I am seeking.

No one wants to be the only available source.

The window is not the view; the window allows the view.

All these people passing by. Every year another ocean of faces I will never see again. By using my eyes I can connect with a few, but only a few. And even that is often misunderstood.

In a lifetime I will lay eyes on thousands of human beings, across rooms, on the streets, inside buildings. What will come of it? Nothing. Absolutely nothing. Unless I change my attitude, they will remain a part of the dull background.

As I was walking back from Gary's office, I was remembering something funny he had said. Several people had passed me before I realized that all of them had smiled when they had seen my face. This shows me a possibility of some general yet satisfying kind of stranger-to-stranger communication. I'm sure it's not to be found in rehearsed greetings or a prescribed sweetness of expression. It is most probably a component of those mental states such as humor, love, happiness, which, without trying, already includes the people one will meet.

However fatuously arrived at, even if it's that we look into each other's eyes as we pass in the aisle of a store, something is formed by this crossing of two lives. For a moment a new mixture has been made. No matter how quickly done, I hand something over.

Coming home today I was in a five o'clock line of cars that was driving down Paseo de Peralta. There was a little boy sitting on an adobe wall who was having the time of his life waving at each driver that went by. I didn't see one person who could refuse him.

I tried an experiment today. I walked around the plaza holding the thought that I had returned home but that my appearance was so radically changed no one could recognize me. All these people used to be very good friends of mine, and I was amused and delighted to see them again and to discover how well they were doing. As I walked I maintained this attitude, but I didn't try to force eye contact. What I discovered was that there was one group, more than half, who were oblivious to me, but there was another group who nodded or smiled, and I had a peculiar feeling that they were in on the secret—but that the secret was not what I had thought. The secret was that we were not strangers, that in some tangible sense our relationship had begun before that moment.

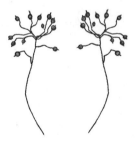

Love sees things as they are. One feels understood by the person who likes him, misunderstood by the person who doesn't—and those feelings are probably realistic.

Except briefly in elementary school I had never played
football, but in my senior year of high school I decided
to try out for the team, partly because I liked the new
coach and partly because I wanted to confront my fear of
contact sports, which I knew at times could be almost
incapacitating. It quickly became clear that the coach
had a much higher opinion of my abilities than I did,
and under his daily urgings I began to transform in a
way that seemed miraculous to me. I not only made the
first team but lettered. He had seen what I was capable
of and would accept nothing less from me. When I went
to college the coach there was indifferent. My fear
returned and I eventually stopped playing altogether.
I had felt the power of being loved but not yet of loving
myself.

There is another way to go through life besides
being pulled through it kicking and screaming.

Learning to love yourself is the definition of change.

Love expands: it not only sees more and enfolds more,
it causes its object to bloom.

When my self-esteem is a veneer, that is, when it stands on superficialities such as body, dress, glibness, reputation, I am less sensitive to other people as people, as living, laughing, hurting human beings. I stop seeing the differences and only watch others for their reactions to me.

Sometimes I wonder if my standard of loyalty for my own
individuality is as high as it is for my friends. I am
capable of selling myself out just to make points.
Where are the decency and fairness for all when I present
myself with anything less than dignity?

I downgrade myself in order to please, but of course it
never pleases. It's not realistic to expect someone to
feel any more respect for me than I display for myself.

If someone has his own respect, it can be seen in his posture, his voice, the integrity of his opinions. But it can't be strategy. And it has nothing to do with formality and restraint, because if one loves himself he can also abandon himself; he can throw himself on the wind because he is safe.

It's pure pleasure to be around Jim and his little boy.
No one could miss seeing how much they love each other.
Even their most petulant arguments are touched with
gentleness. Love isn't a war I'm engaged in. If I truly
like someone, my affection will be recognized. When Gayle
is on the phone it is clear from her laugh, her tone of
voice, how much she likes the person at the other end.
One uses an assiduous pressure in the attempt to convince
someone he is liked more than he is. Love has no need to
show itself off. It can be seen in position. Every muscle,
every gesture, betrays it.

Love is uncovered; it is carefully disrobed, like
folding back petals. It isn't a medal of sainthood.

As soon as they marry, some people get funny ideas about "rights."

I see no point in a marriage in which the overbalancing effort is directed at getting the other person to behave.

The person I want to live my life with is the person to whom I can give the greatest opportunity to do with her life what she wants.

A couple, who for the past nine years have had an almost
ideal relationship, got married this Christmas. It lasted
three weeks. It's not uncommon for a rancorous marriage
to break up and for the people to then live together unmarried
quite harmoniously. In either case, the difference
is often the extent to which the two are willing to let
each other alone.

Marriage isn't mutual ownership. It should be an act of trust in each other's good sense and good intentions. If a marriage is an expression of respect, then it can add grace to love and can temper the momentary selfishnesses that may cause someone to let slip a friendship he has been building for years.

As of July, Gayle and I will have been married twelve years. That means ours will be the longest continuous relationship I have had. I never lived with either of my parents, day in and day out, for that stretch of time. Before we got married I wouldn't have guessed that this simple accumulation of years, taken by itself, would affect the quality of my life. It has given it an added bit of dignity: someone I admire has wanted to spend twelve years of her life with me.

For many years my opinion of marriage was that it tends to be obstructive of growth, that it is a set of externally imposed restraints that often discourage the individual from leaving a relationship that is depleted. My assumption was that no relationship is eternal, that each has its own natural progression and span, and that the aware person can know the time to stay and the time to leave—why then enter into an agreement based only on the ideal of staying? I looked at long-term marriages with suspicion. After all, how much change could ten or twenty years with the same person allow? And when there is little variation, little stimulation, people are predisposed to remain as they are. Now my experience has shown me an alternative, and like many other things that work, it doesn't argue well. I am quite certain that Gayle and I would not be together now if we had not consented to, or had not constructed for ourselves, some type of deterrence to leaving. By getting married, we agreed to try for something lasting; we agreed to rules that would make parting unpleasant; we pledged love, support, and equal sharing of all that we had; and we declared this publicly so that if we failed it would be known. It was not a reasonable thing to do. I remember the night we drove to Oklahoma so that we could get tested and married in two hours. I kept saying to myself, "I'm making a big mistake." Twelve years later I know that my instinct allowed for a possibility that my reason would have precluded.

Whenever I take a long run, I go through one or two periods when my body feels as though it were trying to shut down. If I were to follow its lead I would slow to a walk. Had this consistently been my response when I first began cross-country running, I would never have become conditioned to last for two or more hours, and would not be able to explore out into the badlands every day, and would not have known the experience at other times of having a body with this kind of reserves. I have seen this pattern before. There have been other times when I reached a physical or creative plateau and then overrode what felt like a natural restraint. The results were that I broke into what was for me a new territory (with its own new boundaries).

The next closest thing to a long-term marriage that I have experienced was the mandatory change of roommates we had each ninety days at boarding school. Everything would look the same—the room, the schedule—except suddenly you were living with a stranger. Over the years, that happens in marriage with remarkable regularity. You consider yourself perfectly fine as you are, but all at once this person, whom you thought you had long since figured out, begins to find large sections of your personality unacceptable. And you know that if you want to stay married, you're going to have to change. The type of growth demanded is somewhat unusual, for even though you can see merit in the criticisms, you would be content to stay as you are, and so you find yourself changing in part out of love for someone else. That is often more difficult, but also more satisfying, than essentially self-interested, self-congratulatory improvement.

Love, the magician, knows this little trick whereby two people walk in different directions yet always remain side by side.

Very seldom will a person give up on himself. He continues to have hope because he knows he has the potential for change. He tries again—not just to exist, but to bring about those changes in himself that will make his life worth living. Yet people are very quick to give up on friends, and especially on their spouses, to declare them hopeless, and to either walk away or do nothing more than resign themselves to a bad situation.

I am comfortable around my friend. For reasons not always clear to me, she loves me. She has seen me blunder; she is aware of my annoying self-indulgences, my private habits. All the things I once thought no one could know about me and still love me, she knows. In her presence I have very little to guard against, because she distills me from my words. We have been together a long time, and now some grace within her can see me even when her eyes are open.

the quiet thoughts
of two people a long time in love
touch lightly
like birds nesting in each other's warmth
you will know them by their laughter
but to each other
they speak mostly through their solitude
if they find themselves apart
they may dream of sitting undisturbed
in each other's presence
of wrapping themselves warmly
in each other's ease

The way two people make love summarizes the state of their relationship.

If getting someone to bed against their will becomes one's mission, he may succeed with their body, but in the process he will waste their soul. He will not feel that exchange of spirits after which one walks away having gathered life. He will sense a small death because he has fastened himself onto a cadaver.

Intercourse in which the other person is left out is masturbation, and anyone who has been used in that way knows what it feels like to be a device.

People who fold their clothes neatly and then settle down to business have failed to notice that sex is not sensible.

A few months after I had dropped out of college, I came back on campus to visit an English professor from whom I had taken two courses. Although my wording was somewhat oblique, I succeeded in informing her that I found her attractive and that I thought it would be a good idea if we made love. Teaching me one final lesson, she got out her appointment book and said, "What about a week from Wednesday after my three o'clock class?"

The erotic receives its force not just from acres of
flesh and the sheer weight of bodies, but from the cutting
silver of subtleties: acts begun and not completed, silences
created, words withheld, rhythm building upon rhythm,
startling intrusions, tenderness, and overwhelming waves
of peace. For such magic one must first remove one's head.

Flirting is pure witchery when it works. In just a glance,
a thing almost embarrassing in its intimacy can pass
between strangers. Something from that other world where
everything is known must live inside the eyes.

Sometime after I turned thirty I began for the first
time in my life to get blunt sexual advances, especially
from women in their late twenties to early forties.
Several friends have been quick to assure me I'm not
alone, and the experiences a few of them have had are
instructive. When I was in my teens, the change in tone
when the subject came up (among my male friends) indicated
that sex was considered by all of us to be the motherlode
this side of eternity. The problem was getting it. I
don't recall our having a single discussion on ways to
turn it down. The fact was, unless one privately yearned
to be an ascetic, turning it down was an idea our heads did
not have the machinery to process. I now see some men my
age making an awkward mistake. For them, questioning a
woman's motives or attractiveness is still unthinkable—
after all, they have waited so long for such generous
portions—and so you have this burlesque of men being hustled
off to bed, only to uncover, with heroic frequency, the fact
that their bodies, which are no longer dumb and omnivorous,
refuse to be helpful. Wisdom first appears in unexpected places.

Feelings of friendship are almost always mutual, but sexual attraction may or may not be. In most instances we're not entirely certain how the other person feels, especially since so many people come on strongly for other reasons: to tease, to manipulate, to become sought after. So in order to find out, someone is going to have to show his feelings, and that is when he can get hurt. The one who has to find some way to say, No, I don't feel that way about you, is also uncomfortable because he may not want to jeopardize what has been or could be a good friendship, or simply because he doesn't want to make the other person suffer. He may know that being turned down is a wound that can take a long time to heal. I don't know of an easy way out. Honesty from the beginning seems to help, like pulling adhesive from the skin quickly. The times I have suffered least from being rejected have been with women who didn't stop with no, but who went on to show me how strongly they wanted our friendship to continue, who simply would not allow me to believe I was not liked.

Anyone who has had to do battle with his weight has experienced the importunity of hunger. No matter how formal the resolution, how spiritual the intention, how frequent the reminders, there will be occasions when hunger will outdistance him. That isn't a circumstance anyone appears to have much difficulty understanding. However, because it isn't true of them, many people will not consider the possibility that a sex drive can be equally unrelenting. I have yet to meet a man who abstained completely from masturbating when he was an adolescent, even though many have told me they tried. Yet some talk as if a few years later that same drive, now that it entails a partner, has become for every adult a "temptation"—something as simple to eschew as an unaffordable item in a store window. And so they offer substitute explanations for its intensity: "ego" or "proving one's masculinity" or "regaining one's youth." To argue against the need is futile. The fact is that people differ in their sexual desires, and for some, abstinence is not an alternative. What can be tempered is the manner in which ones finds release. The sexual instinct doesn't include a necessity to let oneself be used or humiliated, nor does it require that one trample on friendships just so that every feasible partner can be pursued.

The problem with infidelity is that it doesn't feel like infidelity. It isn't ill will against a third person; it's "I want to" with this person. The "disloyalty" has to be reasoned out. I reason that this is an act of aggression as well as an act of love, but I don't feel it.

The feeling of disloyalty comes when I tell my partner I have made love with someone else. That's when she suffers. And I deserve the feeling because I am responsible for her suffering: I knew in advance what her reaction would be. So what has my confession gained? Is it that I can walk away saying I have been an honest man? Is that what I have been?

Today at lunch a friend told me she was furious at her husband. He had called to tell her that he had to make a business trip to Charlottesville but he wanted her to know that while he was there he would not visit his former wife. My friend said, "The day he arrives is the date of his daughter's birthday. He never misses a birthday. If he was going to lie to me he could have at least had the decency to make it convincing."

I know a man who talks about honesty as if it were an
absolute. If he holds nothing back from his wife, and if
what he says is accurate, then in his mind he has been
honest. However, there are two parts to communication: what
is said and what is heard. And since one of the concerns
of honest communication is to become closer by partaking
more deeply of each other's thoughts and feelings, it is
important to recognize that sexual attraction for someone
outside the relationship is a subject that suggests a
lessening or even the abandonment of closeness. It
doesn't surprise me that this man complains of his wife's
repeated overreactions. Of course she reads more into his
disclaimers than he states. So would I. If I were told,
"Yes, I slept with him, but it didn't mean a thing," that
is not all I would hear. I would hear what else I know
about infatuation: that it's not always within a person's
control, that it can appear to be over when in fact it
is not, and that it sometimes carries its subject away.
Because sexual attraction has within it the possibility
for sweeping and irretrievable change, the constant
reporting of every symptom of it has the potential for
excruciating torture.

When making love, people instinctively do what they want
done. They eventually touch their partners where or in
the manner they themselves want to be touched, or they
find a way to tuck the subject into the conversation.
At Romona's party I noticed that something similar takes
place between two people who have just met. The person
who wants to be precious will ask adoring questions.
Someone waiting to tell you about his work will ask you
what you do. There was a gallery owner taking very good
care of his respectability; his words touched everyone
with proper coolness. And a woman who wanted me to look
at her considerable intellect poured facts all over me.

Just in case I missed it from the way he dressed, his vocabulary, the subjects he was versed in, a man spent a lot of time this afternoon telling me who he was. And he found me a willing believer. Consequently, we parted having never met. A person is not a millionaire, or a priest, or a dog trainer, or anything else besides a person, no matter if he wears the uniform and plays the role to the hilt. Just like me, he came from his mother's womb covered with blood and mucus.

The introvert has no advantage on the extrovert. It works either way. As a person grows to like himself, he becomes more tolerant of others. If a person gains a new appreciation of someone else, that pulls with it his opinion of himself.

A human is too complex to be taken in whole, to be seen in all his parts, to be assessed in a moment. Even if it were possible, an instant later his mood has changed, he has remembered some act of kindness or humiliation, or a thing unseen has poured into him, even as it has into the eyes that judge him.

It took me a while, but after I had mentally stripped
him of all his gold and white silks and his retinue of
secretaries, I saw he was just another overweight,
middle-aged man. From his eyes, which were peeking at
me from beneath all that power and opulence, I could tell
he was having a great time being God's burning presence
to all these people swarming through my house, and now
that I saw what he was, I could be in on his fun, and I
was free to like him.

In order to point my finger in praise or deprecation,
in order to know some quality whether it is sweet or
sour, in order to recognize it, that characteristic
must in some way reside in me.

It isn't possible to be enlightened and know it.
What you hold yourself superior to is a part of you.

The character of a church, a business or a government can be seen in its attitude toward its detractors.

Friends eventually forgive and come back together because people need people more than they need pride.

Most of us don't look at things, we look at aspects of things. Our interests are specific. We don't see people, we see clothes or bodies or mirrors of our performance, or we see symptoms of wealth or grace or intellect or sensuality. And slowly we become what we look at most.

Thought directs the eyes and eyes direct the soul.

One of the things I don't like about myself is my
capacity for dismissing certain people. I did it again
tonight. I was introduced to a man who instead of
saying, "Hello," said, "Peace," and I thought, Oh God
another one of those. On the spot I wrote him off.
On what possible grounds can I judge someone that
quickly? I know this is the same quality in me that
on other occasions makes me squirm with inferiority.

There may be some people who should be removed from my life the instant they enter it. However, there's a difference between my dismissing a person because I am being controlled by some mindless, reflexive bias, and ridding my life of an individual whom I can see—because I am looking at him—bears me no good will.

There is always a person around who needs the illusion of rising by putting someone else down. The interesting thing about this type of exchange is that the one who is getting worked over usually doesn't realize it. That happened tonight at Nat's slide show. Dewey was getting it good from a man I had never met, and everyone knew it except Dewey, who, with almost touching earnestness, kept setting himself up. There is a surprisingly widespread disbelief in malice. No one likes to think he can be readily disliked; nevertheless, someone who has a general desire to make others feel ill at ease doesn't need good reason. In any group of people there is usually as much effort being directed at causing discomfort as there is straightforward support.

I am having to scrub down the opinion I have of every friend of mine Langley has met. I sit here listening to him analyze people I have known for years, and it's like being fed a kind of slow poison. I realize his criticisms are mostly accurate, but the effect is to magnify their failings and so disfigure them that by the time he is finished, my good opinion of them has lessened. I think I am probably betraying them by even listening: it clearly feels that way.

I'm fond of Langley. He is eloquently droll and consistently unboring. Yet I almost always come away not liking myself. Because of his wit I hesitate to connect him with this aftertaste, but I know other people who can affect me the opposite way: I have left them feeling I have been set in flight, or handed something old of great value. I am naive to think he could wish the best for me when he is so embittered toward everyone else. If being around a person of good will is refreshing, then this generalized ill will can cause me to feel diminished.

If I feel "no," if my entire being is telling me "no,"
then the only thing I can lose by saying "no" out loud
is clutter—just one less person who isn't really a
friend.

All these social lies. Do I have to hide the truth?
I'm treating my friends as if they can't be trusted. If
I say it honestly, then I'm showing confidence in their
willingness to understand; I'm treating them as friends.
I don't think most people are fooled anyway. Somewhere
inside them they sense that they are not being confided in.

Live as if everything you do will eventually be known.

In what order are the souls ranked today? All morning,
I have been receiving calls: "What did so-and-so mean by
that?"—"Why wasn't I invited?"—"What did she say, what
did she say?"—"I thought we were their best friends."
I have lost my tolerance for intrigue. It is a demeaning
waste of time. Friendship can't result from brilliant
footwork. Here you've plotted and sweated and schemed
and now you're considered by everyone to be his best
friend—does that make the time you spend with him one
bit more enjoyable?

A curious reciprocity runs through most aspects of human relationship. Canceled engagements and turned-down invitations are an example. If it isn't suitable for one, more often than not the change in plans works out best for the other. There is no obvious reason why this should be true, and my inclination is to be displeased without waiting to see what effect the change will have.

We were having dinner. I asked Gene if that was his
friend John R. who just walked in. He said yes.
"Aren't you going to speak to him?" "No," he said. "I
never speak to anyone in public. All that happens is
you ask oily, nimble-footed questions about each other's
imaginary lives. And you know the most you're going to
get is a weather report. It tires me out because I'm no
good at social skills. I've told everyone I'm nearsighted."

Recently two friends have gone on vacations. I had had a good visit with one of them a week before he was to leave, and also the other one, about a week and a half before. The first asked that we get together one last time. We did, and the occasion was a little dull and perfunctory. But I hadn't learned the lesson. I suggested to the second friend that he drop by and see me before he left, which he did, and our time together had the chill of exchanged greeting cards in December.

So often I worry about a decision before it has to be made. I will always know more than I do now about both the situation and my own feelings, when the time comes to decide. And interestingly, one recurring phenomenon is that the very information needed to make the best choice often doesn't arrive until it is time for a decision.

Honesty can be gentle—that's what so much of this popularized bluntness lacks, this everything-gut-level, this point-blank-on-all-occasions. It is humorless posturing, a mode of superiority, and it's exhausting to be around. I want to be honest out of respect. And if I must lie in order to spare someone senseless pain, then it is my responsibility to lie so well that it won't be given a second thought.

If we knew everything that was ever said about us and if at the same time we took every word at face value, we would remain friends with no one.

When one is critical of a third person, often he is not convinced; he says it for the effect it will have on the people he is with—a form of posing or a way to confide.

It's becoming clear to me that no one fully knows what he is saying. In conversation we don't have the luxury of a rough draft. Just take a good look at someone trying to talk: every time he opens his mouth it's an experiment and a gamble, often a minor disaster. His friends are the ones who don't hold it against him. Even if one had unlimited time to word each thought, there is no fact or feeling so obvious, so simple, that it would fit perfectly into a sentence.

It's not how much I've been mistreated, but my fear of suffering, my headlong flight from the pain, that makes me callous.

I hurt because I have been refusing to bend. Pain **breaks** me down so that I can be reshaped. If it's really pain, if it has come to that, then there is no getting out of it. Nothing I do works. It will grip me until I am transformed.

Pain must never be taken philosophically; otherwise it isn't pain, we haven't been opened up. The more human we become the more likely we are to suffer. Approachable means vulnerable, woundable, not made hard by a history of abuse, but like old leather, made softer, more comfortable to be near.

I can be inspired to grow, but more often I grow because I have been broken by certain unyielding realities. When I have once again been made aware of my fallibility, I am then predisposed to learn.

There is a time to let things happen and a time to make things happen.

No one becomes permanently comfortable. Life is not solved. Like a large hibernating animal it turns on its belly and once again we have to crawl out from under it. If we don't move, we die.

If it is not given me to know the course of time, then the best I can do for myself is to be attentive, to watch carefully what is happening, to feel out the direction, to sense what movement I can. It's like trying to work my way along a wall in the dark: It doesn't serve me to turn and rail against the wall. It may even have been placed there for my protection.

One element of maturity is the realization that we don't get away with anything. Any advantage gained or convenience taken, any private procrastination or insincerity, no matter how subtle or quick in passing, is paid for. Not dramatically. Often not noticeably. But enough that we learn, eventually, it is not worth it.

Progress is dirty business. We are taught the smell of the reward.

If every problem must be worked through, if it's true I will not be saved by the bell, that death will not release me of a single necessity, then I want to stop, now, putting off what I know must eventually be dealt with.

We are born into a life. The life is waiting there.
We don't pick it, we step into it: parents, first born
or last, the part of the country, the part of the world,
our appearance, the efficiency of our brain. Then a
time comes when we realize that we also have choices,
and so we start the task of building our own life—an
impossible task considering the number of days we are
given to complete it. However, I don't think that's
important; what is important is to begin.

Last night Rusty pointed out a waitress who was taking
orders at the next table. He said that four years ago
she was married, had a fourteen-year-old daughter, and
was the school system's consultant on dyslexia. It was
summer. She and her husband were having a drink in a
bar in Aransas Pass. Her husband went to the rest room
and while he was gone a man at the other end of the bar
said, "Hi. Would you like to come with me to Mexico?"
On the spot she walked out. She lived with the man for
three years in Guatemala. Even more unexpected than the
story was the reaction at our table. We were all staring
at the woman as if she were a heroine. A time comes when
you need to clean house. No, you need to go even further,
you need to burn the house down with yourself inside it.
Then you must walk from the fire and say, I have no name.

Yes there are other considerations. There is no end to
the considerations: feelings of the people involved,
your word, your commitments, the possible consequences.
But a time can come when there isn't much of you left,
and all you have is enough strength to act, just enough
to put an end to it by turning your back and walking out.

I can't help people by damaging myself. In fact, if
it's beginning to destroy me, I can be confident it's
not helping them.

There is something to be said for writing out my beliefs just so I can question them. There is something to be said for setting down the pattern of my life just so I can break with it.

Just because it's what you do best doesn't mean you have to do it.

I have finished reading several accounts of possession
and I'm intrigued with one of the ramifications. The old
personality leaves and a new personality takes over the
old body. Now, if I were the new occupant and today I were
moving into this person called Hugh Prather, I would make
a sign out of precious metal and hang it around his neck;
it would say, UNDER NEW MANAGEMENT. I would have
nothing to lose; no tired uninspired relationships that must be
maintained for God knows what reason; no habits—dressing
habits, eating habits; no pampered tastes; no demeanor to
preserve. I could make new friends or revive old
relationships (because I would have no pride to protect).
I could throw off any mannerism, take up any endeavor,
study any subject, move anywhere—the world would be my
campground.

Joe Osmond was once in a coma for two months. After he came out of it, he rested a few more days in the hospital and then resumed his life. "Nothing had changed," he said. "We think the details are so important. But it's worth noting how much of it simply does not have to get done."

When I lose my sensitivity to those quiet seepages from the other side of reality, my world becomes stubborn and flat and I notice a lack of balance in most of the activities I undertake. A few weeks ago I decided to look for more deliberate ways to attach myself to that other side, and I began to experiment with precognition. On any given day there are numerous opportunities to make a prediction: someone is coming—what time will he arrive? the phone rings—who is it? you make a call—will the person be there? I started out by simply asking a question (for example, what team will win?). The results were no better than if I had guessed. Then I tried seeing the future incident, the way you might try to see what the person who just left had been wearing. I had the least success with numbers (e.g., exact scores), but when I tried picturing the people involved, for instance two of the contestants and their emotional states immediately after a match, and from that picture deducing who had won, I got nearly perfect results. In the Ali-Frazier fight I saw Frazier sitting and Ali standing and interpreted that as Ali's win, although I didn't understand until the fight ended why Frazier would be sitting. In trying to determine if someone is home before I call, I picture the house and mentally go through each room. I usually get a firm impression of whether or not the house is empty. It is not altogether surprising to me that I can sense the mental states of specific people more clearly than the answers to abstract questions. The aspect of the future that I will experience most strongly (and which will therefore stand out most clearly) will be human and complex rather than numerical and precise.

This afternoon I started telling two of my relatives about my experience with precognition. They didn't want to hear about it. They told me that parapsychology was the work of the devil. I've encountered this attitude before. It has always come from people of a similar religious belief. They quote the same biblical passages, which indicates that their conclusions have been shared and not arrived at individually. Why do most humans feel an urge to receive their attitudes from someone else? It's as if we don't want our own minds. I remember when I first moved here I was told by several people that the piñon jays were obnoxious birds. I tried to see them that way, but late in the summer finally succumbed to my own unsophisticated view that they were hilariously preposterous. What interests me is that I would attempt to react as I had been told. The majority's opinion, especially if it's negative, is assumed to be more intelligent. This may come in part from the distrust we learn as children in the accuracy of our own judgment. As adults I believe there is not much pleasure in it, unless it's in the feeling of community.

I have been working on the finish carpentry in the kitchen. Today was my first time to make and set drawers. I noticed that as I got about halfway through each new phase of the work, I was thinking to myself, "It's never as easy as it looks." I didn't like my mental state, even if it was honest, so I decided to be phony and say over and over, "It's always easier than it looks." As soon as I began this, the work became less difficult. It was as if someone had injected me with a vial of knowledge on how to make drawers.

After dinner Oliver came over and sat next to Mr. Mayer, who was across the room from me on the couch. They introduced themselves, then I watched that miracle that sometimes happens when two people come together and at once their minds synchronize. That has happened to me, and there are times when I feel myself striving to bring it about again, especially if I am talking to someone I have just met. When it comes unforced, the phenomenon is almost supernatural. As in some moments of love, there is a feeling of each of us being totally contained within the other. I begin surprising myself with what I say. I state insights that an instant before I didn't know I was capable of. Were they always inside me, but now this person is pulling them out? It feels more nearly as if together we have formed a new mind which until that moment did not exist.

There are moments when I feel that something else is going on, something I knew a long time ago, as though there were once a time when I knew what was behind all of this but now I have forgotten. Sometimes when I wake from a dream it seems I am almost remembering it, or I hear it in the respiration of the waves or see it in the stars when they're so heavy that's all you can look at; even during the instant of stillness when my car was skidding broadside off the road. Throughout my life I have kept returning to that same sense of familiarity. The opposite of a nameless fear. At times I think I am looking down at myself, vaguely recalling that all this shouldn't be taken too seriously, an almost certain conviction that I am not that thing walking around down there.

Here is this other reality about which very little is
said. It is unavoidable but somehow we manage. Only
in retrospect will we touch it. When someone finally
sees it plainly, so plainly that the vision itself will
not allow him to proceed with his life, but stands waiting
for him behind every convenient corner, he quickly
formulates a system designed to transform human personality
and to revolutionize the world. Of course it never does.
It only boxes a corpse. The truth cannot be tidied up.
When it is overstated, intelligent people dismiss it and
then stop looking at even those small but persistent
evidences within their own lives. They continue their
conversations as if there were only a single dimension,
as if everything grew out of the one flat piece of soil
they stand on, as if they didn't die, didn't dream, didn't
wake up in the night screaming, didn't reach for the
phone knowing, didn't feel their diseases melt from them
in the presence of the one they love, didn't sense their
child calling to them, didn't see their friends walk
whole before them in their deaths.

The differing natures of day and night can't be explained by the absence of light. Something moves at night. There is a presence. The demons come out, but so do the Muses.

It happened again this morning: I woke up and for a few seconds I didn't know who or where I was. It seems evident that a filtering or separating process takes place during sleep. My name, location, age, sex, etc., were not present; they had to re-enter my mind. I had been stripped of all the seemingly essential who-are-you, what-are-you answers. I didn't know what I had been doing or what I was going to do, and yet I had a clear sense of continuation, of being, of ongoing existence. I was not panicked; I did not feel newborn; I was familiar to myself. And for the moment that vivid and very personal awareness was all that I had, all that I wanted. Whenever the state has lasted more than a few seconds, I have felt panicked, but the fear always accompanies the start of certain memories, e.g., I know this room but I don't know my name. Many times I have awakened and a moment later the first thing to enter my mind is a feeling of doom or elation. Then the memory follows that explains why I feel that way: the day before my grandfather died, or I received a letter of acceptance from a publisher, etc. There is an apparent order in which the previous contents re-enter my mind. First the emotion, then the incident (dreams are also continually descending those same two steps). Even more fascinating is the pattern: first the location, then the identity. I am here therefore I am Hugh Prather (ah, but one night, unknown to me, my enemies carry me from my bed and float me out into the third ring of Saturn, and then who am I?).

Ontogeny recapitulates phylogeny, but so does one night's dreaming. The mind roams up and down the ages, wanders into other minds, disregards the boundaries of future and past. I close my eyes and hear voices, but I am coming into the middle of something. A conversation is in progress. The participants are indifferent to my arrival. One of them is me. I was having this other conversation and didn't know it.

The second day out of Santa Fe I woke up in the motel but the dream I had been having did not stop. Even though I was fully awake, it continued its progression sharp and undiminished for a period of I would say seven or eight seconds. If I add this experience to the apparent random manner in which my mind steps into a dream, the conclusion I come to is that the dream world or the dreaming mind is ongoing. It is reached through sleep but it is not activated by sleep. My present sense of it is that even at this moment it is acting out its commentary, its allegorical parody, of my relationship to myself and to a profusion of other lives and even to the entire sweep of time. At any given instant during the day, I am probably causing new eddies of dream stories that, if I knew how, I could see as clearly as I see the tracks I leave behind in an arroyo.

There have been other nights like this one when I have
awakened knowing that I have been fighting with something
for hours. A terrible struggle with something. I am
exhausted. I have won—I know that because I am here,
but I know too that it will come again.

My dreams, my nighttime battles, tell me unequivocally
that I want to be good. I am trying, God knows I am
trying, to wash off this slime of self-betrayal.

I know of no more deadly state of mind than the one in which I become preoccupied with possessions. Every time I start comparing my house, clothes, car, income against those of my friends, I feel my personality twisting into a deformity. There will always be those who will do better than I and those who will not, and no other fact could be more irrelevant to life's meaning.

I am continually underestimating my capacity for selfishness. I like to think of myself as generous, especially
toward my friends, but I'll suddenly see new uses for
some old possession I am about to give away, or in the
middle of a favor—that I have offered to do—I begin
resenting the time it is taking. I wish I weren't
afraid. I wish I could loosen my grip and enjoy this
very simple pleasure of giving.

I can't throw off the habits of a lifetime. To attempt
to do so is to lose ground. It's a question of which
way to look. In a marathon the man in second place is
usually the one who looks over his shoulder. So long
as I am doing battle with my many immaturities, I am
not allowing myself to grow up. Why become engaged
with sweeping my path of old footsteps when I can take
one new one?

Life is not just, even though our sense of justice is
one part of life. Yet if we abandon our personal sense
of right and wrong because it's not the standard by which
reptiles and insects operate, we betray ourselves and so
become an enemy to our own substance. The paradox is
that although life is not righteous, we can make
peace with our life only through righteousness.

Stands must be taken. If I am to respect myself I have to search myself for what I believe is right and take a stand on what I find. Otherwise I have not gathered together what I have been given; I have not embraced what I have learned; I lack my own conviction.

I visited the free school today. After classes one of
the instructors and I took a station wagon full of eight-
to thirteen-year-old boys out to a construction site.
Lining the foundation excavation were mounds of dirt
ranging in height from ten to fifty feet. The instructor
had come to pick up a backhoe, and while he worked on
starting it, I watched the boys play on the mounds.
They started jumping off the lower ones and then began to
move up in height. Three of the boys progressed very
quickly, but I was impressed with the seriousness of one
of the boys who did not. Even though it had already been
tried by the others, he began working on overcoming his
fear of jumping off one of the smaller hills. I could
see the struggle in his face. The most he could expect
would be a victory over himself, and that is what he
accomplished; then he went on to the next hill, seemingly
unmindful of the calls of "Big deal!" from the other boys.

Four years ago I set out to build my own house. I worked for one year and during that time most of what I was doing was interesting and challenging. I continued the second year and was now giving directions to the men and women who were helping me. New relationships were formed. I was busy, and tired at the end of the day. Anyone could see the results of my labor. My work still had the look and feel of a meaningful endeavor, but the fact was it had ceased to challenge me. There are a surprising number of activities like that. They have all the trappings of importance. Their luster is further enhanced by the respect in which society holds them. A woman will state with pride that she is going to have a baby. Every week a man will have a new story about how badly he has been mistreated. A couple will make the rounds announcing that they are getting married. Someone else will describe in detail the times he was so sick he almost died. These pronouncements are usually reacted to as if they were accomplishments (even endless conversations about tragedies—deaths, accidents, murders—will generally be listened to with respect). But none of these are in themselves a meaningful way to be occupied. They can break the status quo and fill up our days, but they are still only what we make of them.

It's obvious that many of the problems I have are the result of how things were when I was growing up. So here I am spending the rest of my life suffering for personality traits I never asked for. Where is the justice in that? There isn't any. But I was never promised justice.

Maybe we are deluding ourselves with all our theories of growth and techniques of improvement. Maybe the truth is that progress is beyond our comprehension, but since that fact is unbearable, we busy ourselves with endeavor. We read articles, we listen to authorities, we have insightful discussions, and yet I wonder if we have any real idea of where we are headed. Maybe we cannot alter the path of our lives. If we were allowed to walk in the direction we seek to walk, maybe it would be a disaster. When I look at myself at thirteen, or at eighteen, or even at twenty-five, I see that I had no grasp of the principal changes that were occurring in my life. What I believed, the books I read, the concepts I spouted, were mostly beside the point. Now I think that I have at least a partial image of the overall pattern of my life. I believe it is possible for me to act in a way that will affect positively, if not the outcome, then the character, of my life. But I also believed that then.

I used to act as if I were racing after some magical thought. No new system could be left unbelieved. I swallowed whole every supposition fed to me. Anything was acceptable so long as it was unprovable. It was as if one day I might think the thought that would break me out. They were up there listening, and if I thought the right thought they would invite me up. Then I would sigh and say, "Wasn't that an experience!" They would smile knowingly, and I would be one of them.

If I have to think of something in order to act differently, then no real change has yet taken place.

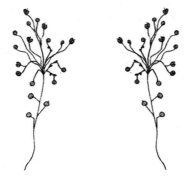

A new idea has energy, but like a new battery in an old five-battery flashlight, its power is temporary. It is natural for me to return to activities that are known, to once again think thoughts that are familiar. To be constantly reminding myself to change requires an effort that cannot be sustained. Nor should it be. The longer I coerce myself to obey a concept that no longer inspires me, the more I must trample my own loves and instincts and natural interests. Nothing is gained by pushing something good beyond its season. An idea can inspire me, but it is not inspiration. I change in spurts, but I change. Each new concept leaves its residue. Each idea that excites me to temporary change does in fact permanently change me, even though almost imperceptibly. I will be fortunate if I learn, really learn, one or two lessons in my life. The implication, of course, is that there is more to come.

An honest person does not find himself in agreement with every enumerated belief held by the group of which he is a member.

If I don't take what I read or what I am told and weigh it against my own experience, then of what value am I to myself?

As our experience teaches us the reliability of our own point of view, we begin to entertain the dangerous suspicion that those people out there may not know what they're talking about.

The source is not the thing. One friend is not love. One man's teaching is not salvation.

Time does not separate me from the future in absolute, either-or terms. The present and the future are more like record grooves side by side. Now the present is playing, but occasionally the needle jumps to the next groove, as it did in yesterday's tennis match when I saw an exact picture of the upcoming point. The experience was not unnatural. I sensed that something like it had happened many times. I suspect it does with everyone. So the future is not only imminent, it is here, it is to be dealt with. And if I am not in some way already in it, I at least have a general idea of those qualities toward which I am evolving.

My circumstances, my fortune good or bad, do not constitute the movement of my life.

The feeling is: I am becoming more like myself. That implies either a potential wholeness or a concurrent wholeness. If in some sense I am already what I am changing into, then possibly I can draw more fully upon that existing state.

When at last I think I have changed, I begin to notice that the change feels familiar, that it is not new, that I can recall other times I have felt or acted this way, at least in part. Then, inevitably, the change begins to dissipate. But in not quite the same way as before. It stays longer this time around, or it leaves more of itself behind.

Change is the return of something once known, something that will not be abandoned. I look down the line of my life and I see it surfacing again and again. I recognize it. I am that thing. I am being put back together.

This special relationship I have presumed. I walk along
talking to "him"—that seems a little ridiculous now.
But not so ridiculous as "it," God the It. To think of
all the empathy, caring, pathos, all the love in the universe
caged inside these puny skulls seems absurd, as if
love were a mutation—we have it, the ants don't. The
bloodless laws of physics nurturing a seed of love into
flower, an aberration on the edge of the universe, a few
embers that long for fire; me, feeling love, insisting
in my dementia that where there is a little there must be
a lot—God the lot. But I believe that. I do not believe
we are freaks.

The talking does something. I pray to God, my friend, and it changes me, if only for a moment. I feel myself siding with what is good in me. I feel cleansed, and I look around with more gentleness. Relationships appear to re-form on a new basis: the gentleness in me seeing the gentleness in others. I sense my own beauty and health, and I see a core of goodness in others. The world dances for a moment. Now, if one can feel it, see it, act it, and time and again has it handed back to him, then he knows it exists. So why am I fighting to believe this?

I keep wanting to use the word "wholeness," but that is
in fact what all this holiness lacks. It is not
complete. There is no falling-down-on-the-floor hilarity,
no sex, no spit, no anger. It is soft and beautiful and
sooner or later I crave something more. The question is
can one have both, both pain and caress, passion and
peace, humor and warmth. That's what I have not been
getting. There is something to be said for a fist in the
stomach. I wouldn't want it as a way of life; I could
never say, now, I want it now. It would have to be
unexpected, unplanned. When you've been without
wounds you know it; as in a dreamless sleep, you yearn
for at least one succubus, one grinning vampire in the
night. So, is that what my God is now—both a knife and
a healing touch?

If there is no God, no all-embracing intelligence and love,
if there are only a few pieces of brain scattered through
the universe and everything else in this cold yawning
vacuum, dead dust, an occasional quantum of light, then
I am only talking to the better side of my own nature,
I am appealing to my own instincts of love and courage.
And there is something to be said for that. But I don't
want to be deluded. If I am talking only to myself then
I want to know that.

It is important not to overstate it, not to argue more than I know. The spiritual can't be caught in a handful of words.

You have to just say it. That's the way it is. It's that way because it's that way.

No one ever gets it right. As long as there are human beings, there will never be one who will get it right. The tendency of the mind is always to huddle over its little pile of bromides, to state things easily, and to make simple nodding movements with the head.

There we were today having another intense little discussion about spiritual reality. Isn't anything sacred to me? If it really means that much, how can I talk about it? Isn't there anything so precious that I simply would not smudge it with a single word?

Of course everything I write is coming out dark. I have spent eight years trying to be honest and my unconscious has finally taken me seriously.

No matter how good things get, my capacity to make myself unhappy is always equal to it.

Here I am taking this beetle outside and a mosquito bites
me on my bald spot. When I was hairy and pubescent I would
never have undertaken such an inglorious rescue. Now my
patch of hard-won compassion is abused.

My hair is coming out. At a reasonable rate. It's giving
me plenty of time to adjust. Now if I had a hair transplant,
would I suspend myself in time? Surgically remove wrinkles
and replace hair, and a person gains aesthetically, but does
he lose something else of value? Is my body a lecture
being delivered to me by the universe that I would be
attempting to censor? Or are these the type questions out
of which non-issues are made?

It is this never-ending, all-American, all-consuming war
against aging that I don't want to get caught up in, this
useless battle to check the advance of every wrinkle.
It is an attempt, like so many others, to not be here.

I observe, partly in horror, that my body is off on some course known only to itself. It never reached the promised plateau. The changes at mid-life are as rapid as they are at puberty. I've been put on a roller coaster. I guess I can either stand up and yell to be let off, or sit back and enjoy it.

This parade of old schoolmates. I can see they have been walking into a terrible wind. I look at them and I know for certain I am going to die.

When you're halfway there, you stop disbelieving in there.

The energy, and the time, I have wasted during my life thinking about my body, worrying about almost every part of it at one period or another: my chin is too long, my neck is not long enough, my nose should be more delicate, etc. Now age is handing me a new set of appearance changes to worry about. It occurred to me this morning, the irony that is probably in store for me is that it was never my body anyway; it was a rented house. Certainly it's true that as I get to know someone well I think of him less as a body. My attention is on something inside the body.

"You have such lovely breasts," I said. "Oh but they used to be higher," she answered. "They used to stand up like this." That is the way we kill ourselves. That is the way we die. All day we are waging these little wars against ourselves. The darkness accumulates in our minds like poison.

"Premature aging"—that phrase gives it away. Aging is OK, but not premature aging. If aging is OK, aging is OK.

Time is recorded on our faces, in our muscles; we see its shadow moving across our childhood friends. What if we saw no passage of time? Then I suspect there would be many areas in which we wouldn't grow; our spirit would remain adolescent.

Am I a body or am I a mind riding a horse named body?

The body can't be forced to live the life of the mind.

I think I would take better care of my body if I knew
for sure it is just a dog and cane.

My body grows older. Young women now call me sir and
Mr. Prather. "But don't you see lovely lady, I'm only
trapped in here. Let's make love, and for one enchanted
moment we will exchange bodies and you will know what I
am."

What we don't know is whether the threescore and ten is about all the time we could profitably use anyway. Given the inescapable boundaries of my life—a male Caucasian, the only child of Virginia and Hugh, possessing all my limbs and certain governing childhood memories—could I really benefit from being that same person for, say, two hundred years?

They said it again: "She's burning the candle at both
ends." "More fire to her," I said. "But Hugh, she's
not going to last long at this rate." That shut me up.
I certainly wouldn't want to be heard calling for early
demise. However, the subject shouldn't have ended
there. True, she may not last long, but is lasting long
the most one can hope for? She's burning at both ends,
but aren't we all? Our mind and muscle smolder even
while we sit clucking at her wild thrashings. She at
least feels something. What is the virtue in being a
piece of kindling, one curled shaving of fury? When it's
all over, when nothing remains but to pull up the sheet,
what will we have to say: "I outlived my friends by 7.4
years"?

They have some woman down at the morgue who can't
be identified. She's been there for over three weeks. I
don't remember Santa Fe ever exerting itself in quite
this way before. Both papers are on it. It seems that
everyone I talk to has it on his mind. The Glorieta
Center has even made a public offer to bury her. I
think we are all slightly horrified that anonymity can
come this quickly.

When you get knocked down, you lie there and you say,
"It's pointless. None of this makes any difference."
And because it is pointless, that truth comforts you
and gives you time to heal. But once you have mended,
the very futility that gave you rest now impels you
to even greater effort. The impossibility of it all:
the certain deterioration and death, the ponderous
broom of history sweeping away all traces of individual
lives, motivates you more than the hope of ten thousand
golden statues or trumpets or coins. It is because it
will eventually mean nothing that you must do it.

Look at all these heroics. Here is my friend Mr. Farrington, eighty-one years old, still saying all he wants out of life is to write novels. His work has diminished in both quality and volume. He hasn't had a successful book in twenty years. But he isn't lying. I know I will feel the same way. He wants to do it, he knows he can still do it, and yet he is wrong. He will never again equal what he did twenty years ago. That, however, will not stop him. He's a member of this species that strains off of two legs just so it can keep its head as far as possible from the ground, and which, even when it knows that the very cells of the brain are shrinking, strives to go on, to create, to achieve, to better itself just one more time.

I have been working on the novel for almost three years
and I have known all along that something is wrong. Now
I see what it is. My aim has been high, the writing has
been good, but the quality of the effort has not been
equal. There was no power, no impelling urgency to my
labor. Now that I have doubled my hours and am attempting
something approximating a daily schedule, I feel more
fully used and more integral to the project, also more
deserving of any good results. It is not relevant that
even though my pace was indifferent, the outcome was
acceptable, because there was a spiritual imbalance. A
sense of justice and merit were missing in the work.

There doesn't appear to be a way to give someone else what you know. Whenever I think I have succeeded in keeping someone from going through one more little hell, the long run proves me wrong. Each person has to learn it all over again for himself.

Now he says he wants to be a writer. But when I
tell him about the groundwork, the years of going
unpublished, the filing cabinet full of false starts
and rejected manuscripts, the four years I have been trying
to complete just one 135 page novel, his eyes drift
and he asks about all the letters and phone calls and
the royalties. He is thinking about the time when the
preliminaries will be over. But the preliminaries are
never over. If it's worth getting there then you never
quite make it. He has the facility and the charm, he
may even have talent, but he lacks a certain infatuation
with toil. He hungers for the goal but not for the
struggle. Writing doesn't differ from his other endeavors
that never succeeded. The obsession has to be with the
process, the act of putting one word down after another.
No one sees you do that, and by the time most people get
around to reading what you have written, you are
preoccupied with the next project and find yourself a
little annoyed with criticism or praise for something
that to you is clearly over and done with.

It wasn't until I was almost thirty-two that I began to believe in death. We were living in Berkeley where I was starting my second year as an unpublished writer. It was about two in the morning and Gayle was asleep. As I lay in bed I was seized with a nearly absolute conviction that I wasn't going to live to see daylight. I got out of bed and went to the living room. I began to think of all that I had not done with my life, the friends I had neglected, things I had made important that were not important, and I started crying. I cried off and on for several hours, and when the sun finally rose I had begun writing. What I wrote, later became the opening pages of my first published book. There had been no apparent reason for me to fear death; I wasn't sick, nor was I in any danger. I think, very simply, the time had come for me to take my dying seriously. We are forced to grow whether we want to or not, and for me that is a comforting fact. It evidences at least one aspect of the workings of the universe that could be compared to human love. In being made to look at my own mortality, I was in some way being cared for, because the result was that I gained respect for the common material of my life and began a more considerate use of the time I had left.

My life will make a statement. When I am on my deathbed,
I will look back and my actions will say, If only he hadn't
rushed, or they will say, He loved what he did, or they
will say, He traded his talent for money. When that moment
comes, I hope I will have given myself the finest I was
capable of. I hope that what I do will make a bed on
which I can take my rest.

Can a life be looked at as one thing, can I see my life
whole, and can I now take it and make it into something
new, a work of grace? What I have to deal with is for
the most part garbage. When I look at it in one sweep,
it is not noble. I have done little more than get by.
As a teenager and as a young man, there were moments when
I yearned to transcend myself, but overall I see no theme.
Like a wind-up toy dropped randomly on the earth, I climb
over one thing only so that I can climb over the next.
Who or what set me in this direction? Nothing did, nothing
but chance. I can at least try to take my life into my
own hands. I can finish well. A painting, a song, a
poem, can transform in the final seconds of composing.
I once saw Maldarelli do it with a sculpture. As he
hammered off the last few chips of alabaster, the bust
started to live; it was dead and it came to life.

More is out there than is here inside. I don't want to
be afraid to believe. I want to long for something. I
don't want to be afraid to stick my hand up and grope
above the clouds. I want to throw myself on my doubts.
One has to be devastated. Time and again one has to be
torn apart by the facts.

Too late for what?

Every great life dares. Like a man or woman of extraordinary beauty, it is almost ugly. Each attempt approaches the grotesque in its reach.

I am old enough. I have been given the lessons. More than needed. More than I have ever used. The time has come for me to put an end to this busy stocking of supplies. I don't require one thing beyond my own counsel. Why should I keep filling myself with new reminders and techniques—it's nothing other than pro-crastination. I can trust myself. I know what to do.

Now is the time to take possession of my life, to start
the impossible, a journey to the limits of my aspirations,
for the first time to step toward my loveliest dream. "If
I had only known then what I know now"—but now I know
enough to begin.

There was a time when love was in my spirit.
It created a pure burning in my eyes, a flame taken from
a star. I could see it pouring like oil onto the shoulders of my
friends. Like light in the dust it was even in my dreams.
But now my thoughts are the thoughts of dogs, and my
struggles are as the wars of insects. My feet are
bloodied, but the direction is known.

The time comes for every man when he knows he is going to die—not from imminent danger; danger is an accident and accidents pass. I am talking of the realization of the very limits you have been given, of the years you have run through, and of just how much of it you have left. The experience is at first horrifying, but after the horror fades, you are left with a perspective by which you can judge the relative worth or pointlessness of the countless activities you are engaged in and that until then you had let pass unexamined. At this point you may, as I did, become quite arbitrary in your refusal to do certain things that before were routine. Now you know it is a question of time, and it is your time, not theirs, you are being asked to give up. But reality eventually forces you to take a second look, and what you see begins to dissolve your selfishness. You see that you are not alone, that your time will not be spent alone, that your life is in fact many lives, and that no matter how determined you are to make it so, your happiness cannot be solitary. What you see is that there is something else as important to you as your own life.

This evening I happened to look out the window just as the sun was setting. Along with a feeling of awe there was the unmistakable sense of being carried away. For that one moment I knew it didn't make any difference that I was going to die. This small life of mine was not important. I belonged to that beauty, and everything was as it should be.